D1566077

The Living Constitution

Landmark
Supreme Court
Decisions

The Living Constitution

Landmark Supreme Court Decisions

Peter Sgroi

Julian Messner
A Division of Simon & Schuster, Inc.
New York

Published by Julian Messner,
A Division of Simon & Schuster, Inc.
Simon & Schuster Building
Rockefeller Center
1230 Avenue of the Americas
New York, New York 10020

JULIAN MESSNER and colophon are
trademarks of Simon & Schuster, Inc.
10 9 8 7 6 5 4 3 2
Manufactured in the United States of America
Design by Sarabande Press

Library of Congress Cataloging-in-Publication Data

Sgroi, Peter P.
The Living Constitution.

Bibliography: p.
Includes index.
Summary: Explores the function and adaptability of
the Constitution through a description and analysis of
three major decisions—Marbury vs. Madison, Dred Scott,
and United States vs. Nixon.
1. United States—Constitutional law—Cases—
Juvenile literature. [1. United States—Constitutional
law] I. Title.
KF4550.Z9S39 1987   342.73'029   86-23521
ISBN 0-671-61972-1   347.30229

To M. J. and Peter
Whom We Will Always Love.

Acknowledgment

My gratitude and appreciation to Jane Steltenpohl, my editor, for her invaluable assistance with the manuscript; to West Nyack Public Library for source material; to Mary Anne, my wife, for her ever-present support.

CONTENTS

Introduction

The Constitution of the United States, with the Bill of Rights, embodies the ideals of our American society. As a people we value freedom of speech, press, assembly, and the exercise of our religious preference. We count on our right to privacy, to a fair trial, the ability to have problems with the government solved. So as a people we have set these ideas down in the world's oldest written constitution. It provides as well for the powers, duties, form and structure of our government. It is the fundamental law of our land.

One might logically think that a document entering its three hundredth year of existence would be out of touch with modern times and should by now be relegated to the scrap pile of history. It could be a relic of the past like the Wright brothers' airplane or Henry Ford's Model T. But the Constitution, although created in 1787, has not remained inflexible in meaning or trapped in eighteenth-century thinking. It is a vibrant, fresh, and living document.

Justice Brennan of the present United States Supreme Court explains how this is possible. The genius of the Constitution, he says, "rests not in any static meaning it may have had in a world that is dead and gone, but the adaptability of its great principles to cope with the current problems and current needs." Brennan adds that the Constitution is "garbed in cloaks of generalities," which serve future generations as guidelines not solutions for their legal problems of the day.

As an example of a permanent guideline, think of mothers who have always told their teenage children to drive safely. In 1780, driving safely in a horse and buggy might mean ten miles an hour. Today with an automobile it might mean fifty miles an hour, but the teen-naut in the year 3000 might have to keep his spaceship down to 345,000 miles an hour. The principle of driving safely still has the same meaning, but it has been adapted to new circumstances.

Commenting on the problem of institutions and laws not going hand in hand with the progress of the human mind, Thomas Jefferson said, "We might as well require a man to wear the coat that fitted him as a boy. . . ."

The Founding Fathers did not want to leave the interpretation of the Constitution to political forces. They thought it would be torn to shreds. The political party in office would interpret the document in a self-serving and self-interested way.

Instead the Founding Fathers through Article 3 of the Constitution made provision for a United States Supreme Court as well as lower federal courts. The Supreme Court was intended to be a court outside the political arena where independent-minded justices, appointed for life, could decide major cases. The justices would thus avoid the consequence of perhaps being voted out of office should they render an unpopular decision. We will see that the Court's record is uneven in the matter of rising above political influence.

Thus it has become particularly the duty of the 104 justices of the United States Supreme Court to shape the meaning of the Constitution. Chief Justice Charles Evans Hughes underscored this point in 1907 when he said: "We are under a Constitution but the Constitution is what the judges say it is." One of our first Chief Justices felt this is how the Constitution was "intended to endure for the ages . . . consequently to be adapted to the various crises of human affairs."

This book is about three particular crises in America's human affairs and the way in which the Supreme Court handled them. These cases took place over almost a two-hundred-year period of time. The first crisis and perhaps the Court's most fundamental dealt with this question: Which branch of the federal government would be the ultimate interpreter of the meaning of the Constitution? Would it be the executive, legislative, or judicial branch? We will see how the Supreme Court in a very aggressive way, through its decision in *Marbury* versus *Madison* in 1803, answered this historic question.

The second crisis we will examine is how the Supreme Court dealt with the question of slavery and the bitter feelings it created in the country. Different parts of the United States, between 1830 and the outbreak of the Civil War, felt strongly about maintaining or eliminating the bondage of human beings. Whichever way the Supreme Court ruled on this case in 1857, it would alienate a major section of the American people. We will see how the Court responded in the Dred Scott decision to this grave and momentous challenge.

The third decision we will consider is the most modern incident. It deals with the Watergate scandal of the 1970s, Presidential tapes and the question of confidentiality within the executive branch. The Supreme Court came to grips again with a case bristling with political interests. This case is called the *United States* versus *Nixon*.

Through these three Supreme Court decisions we can discover how the Court fits into the

American government and the success it has had in rising above political passions of the day. Its ideal is to bring flexibility but permanence to our country's affairs.

The Constitution itself does not change, but the judges who interpret it do. John Marshall, Roger Taney, and Warren Burger, the Chief Justices who led their courts in three different time periods in American history, faced three different tests. Each of their Courts applied the principles of the Constitution in a different way, bringing different results to the country. The Founding Fathers did not intend the words of the Constitution to be a straitjacket for all events — for all times; their wisdom instead produced a living Constitution, which continues to affect the lives of all of us.

I

MARBURY

VERSUS

MADISON

Hamilton and Jefferson

There were deep-seated differences between various political groups in our country's early history. These differences appeared simultaneously with the creation of the new government under our first President, George Washington.

With the creation of a new government, a great many national issues surfaced and were addressed—some needing immediate answers. Various groups began to present their side of the argument and possible solutions.

Within Washington's cabinet were two unusually intelligent and ambitious men, Thomas Jefferson and Alexander Hamilton. The former served as Secretary of State and the latter as Secretary of the Treasury. They disagreed quite often. Hamilton, at thirty-four years of age, was Washington's youngest appointee, a man of sharp intellect and unquestioned personal honesty. He was a northerner and a city man who favored the particular interests of those groups. Hamilton was skeptical of the judgment of the "turbulent and changing masses."

Thomas Jefferson, on the other hand, came from what was then a southwestern farm area. Unusually brilliant in many fields, he had a rich knowledge of the writings of French and English political thinkers. He was the author of the Declaration of Independence. Jefferson believed the people's judgment could be trusted. He was not afraid of democracy but felt it was a practical necessity or civilization would come to a halt.

Hamilton, as America's premier economic genius, believed if America was to survive economically it would need a strong upper class. Hamilton also wished to organize the country on a national scale and promote trade and commerce. Jefferson was afraid that a strong central government would become too powerful and therefore dangerous. Cities would corrupt and complicate society, he worried. Farmers, "those who labor in the earth," he felt were the chosen people of God, if he ever had a chosen people. The people at the local and state level should resolve their own problems and not rely on the national government.

In foreign affairs the two also took opposite points of view. Jefferson thought English society immoral and decadent. Hamilton admired the orderliness of the British government and created a financial program for the United States based on the British model. The French Revolution horrified Hamilton because of the violence and social disruption. Jefferson felt it was another blow against tyranny and a triumph for democracy.

The conflict between these two men widened slowly. At first the Secretary of State supported Hamilton's financial plan during Washington's administration. Both agreed it was wise for the national government to pay its debts. These debts were owed our foreign allies who helped our country win the American Revolution. There were state and national debts as well. But when Hamilton proposed taxing the farmers with a whiskey tax and creating a national bank, Jefferson could not go along. Jefferson felt these measures were designed to benefit the northeast commercial class at the expense of the southern planter and western farmer.

Many more people with similar beliefs began to side with these two personalities, and political parties appeared on the scene.

The Need for a Party System

The Constitution of the United States called for a republican form of government. The people qualified to vote, usually those who met property requirements, were to elect a President and members of the House of Representatives. In order to gain control of the government and to put across their own political program, leaders in public affairs needed to fill these offices with loyal, similar-thinking people. Political parties made this possible. They served to frame issues for the voters, to select candidates for office, and to help them be elected. The party also acted as a watchdog when the other parties were in office. In the early days of our government a great deal of this organizing was in the testing and experimental stage. Gradually America's first two political parties emerged. The Federalist Party was led by Alexander Hamilton and reflected his views on the importance of a strong central, or federal, government. The other leading party was the Democratic-Republican Party, directed by Thomas Jefferson and emphasizing the interests of the small farmer and the values of the common people.

At times each political party took an extreme view of the other. The Federalists feared that Jefferson's party wanted mob rule. The Democratic-Republicans feared Hamilton's followers would run the country for the benefit only of the rich, able, and wellborn.

This situation became explosive at times. So

much so that in his Farewell Address, Washington urged the people to avoid party factions because "this spirit of party" would have harmful effects on the country.

The Election of 1800

The Presidential election of 1800 represented the first time that America changed political parties. The Federalist Party with its resources of talent and ability had given the country sound financial stability and kept us out of war. It prevented anarchy and strengthened the new national government. The Federalists were fearful that the incoming Jeffersonian Party would destroy the Constitution and create a new social order, resulting in utter chaos for the country.

The election campaign was a bitter and vicious one. It reflected the deep-seated differences between these two political groups. A great deal of name-calling and outright lies had appeared in newspapers and pamphlets.

When Thomas Jefferson won the election, feelings ran so high that his opponent, Federalist President John Adams, left town. He refused to witness his successor take office on March 4, 1801. John Adams actually believed our country's days were numbered once Jefferson took over as head of state. The outgoing President considered Jefferson a fanatic.

Jefferson's Inaugural Address

In his Inaugural Address Thomas Jefferson pleaded for political tolerance. He exclaimed at one point in his speech: "We are all Republicans; we are all Federalists." But the outgoing party did not believe him. John Marshall, the newly appointed Chief Justice of the United States Supreme Court, had, as his very first duty, sworn in the new President. He was himself a moderate Federalist and was ultimately to be the center of a future controversy with Jefferson. The very morning of the Inauguration he wrote: "The Democrats are divided into speculative theorists and absolute terrorists. With the latter I am disposed to class Mr. Jefferson."

The Congressional election of 1800 gave an emphatic majority to the Democratic-Republicans as well. This party had now won control over the executive and legislative branches of the national government. This left the judicial branch as the only stronghold of the rival party.

The Role of the Courts

During the early part of our history, as they do today, courts played a vital role in the everyday life of the ordinary citizen. Americans were a mobile society—always on the move—and land claims produced inevitable disputes. Businesses were growing quickly, and legal questions about bankruptcies, collections of debts, making or breaking contracts came up quite often. The state courts were often manned by judges who were the defendants' friends and neighbors.

The Judiciary Act of 1789 had provided for the creation of the new national court system in addition to the already existing state courts. It was this act that created the United States Supreme Court, as well as district courts and courts of appeal. These national courts handled out-of-state suits, cases involving federal law, including non-payment of federal taxes. The past two Federalist Presidential administrations had filled many of the judicial posts with their own party members.

Federal Judges

The judges on these federal courts were almost always "foreigners"—out-of-staters who often lacked understanding of local conditions. Some of them bullied the litigants and jurors, as well as being vulgar and prejudiced. On many an occasion these judges would make political speeches to the juries—that is, lecture them on how terrible the Republican Party was instead of keeping strictly to the business of justice. But what irritated Jefferson even more than the politicizing of this court system was the application of the English common law to cases. Jefferson was not an Anglophile and did not accept the theory that where Congress had not passed a law covering the handling of a legal dispute, judges should be guided by cases based on old English practices and tradition. Americans, he believed, had forcibly rejected anything English through their Revolution against the mother country. And yet these Federalist federal judges applied this sometimes harsher common law and many times stifled freedom of thought, assembly, and expression. The English law was especially hard on debtors, defaulters, and bankruptcies. What made matters even worse was that these federal judges were appointed for life.

Jefferson could not wait to do something about the court situation. But the Constitution did not permit him to take office until March 1, 1801 (the allowance for travel time was considerably greater then than provided for today). During this four-month "lame duck" interim with the President-Elect forced to wait on the sidelines, the Federalists rammed through Congress the self-serving Judiciary Act of 1801. But what infuriated an already impatient Jefferson was the audacity of President Adams' appointment of a Federalist as Chief Justice of the United States Supreme Court.

The Appointment
of John Marshall

In December of 1800 President Adams received a letter from Oliver Ellsworth, the Chief Justice of the Supreme Court, resigning his office claiming "affliction with the gravel and the gout and intending to pass the winter in the south of France." John Marshall, Adams' Secretary of State, who enjoyed the high esteem of the President, suggested he appoint Justice William Paterson of New Jersey in Ellsworth's place. Adams instead offered the post to John Jay of New York.

Jay had been Washington's appointment as Chief Justice but had quit the Court six years before. At that time the Supreme Court as an institution was considered a laughing matter by politicians. So insignificant was the Court that when Washington, DC, the capital of the United States, was planned a place was provided for the President and Congress but none for the Supreme Court. The Supreme Court met in a committee room lent to it by the Senate.

In the years Jay presided the Court ruled on merely two cases and met only twice a year for a few days. It was difficult to find men to serve on the High Court. In addition, the Court at this point in time lacked a clear-cut function.

John Marshall was almost certain John Jay would turn down the appointment. Jay, he surmised, at his age, could not possibly survive the rigors of riding circuit.

Riding Circuit

By an act of Congress each Supreme Court member was assigned an area, or circuit, in which he heard cases. The judges divided into pairs and rode within these large areas, from federal court to federal court, twice a year. At each stop they joined a federal district court judge and held court. The judges had to spend months traveling over unfinished roads in horse-drawn carriages or on horseback, passing their nights in crowded, smelly taverns. In addition to the physical strain this duty put on the aging members of the High Court, if the lower court cases were appealed, the same judges would have to listen again to the same cases.

While waiting for John Jay's reply to President Adams' offer of the position of Chief Justice of the Supreme Court, John Marshall persuaded the President to do away with the circuit duties. Adams agreed, and in his last message to the "lame-duck" or outgoing Congress he recommended a reform bill called the Judiciary Act of 1801.

Shortly before January 20, 1801, John Jay answered the President's request. Jay declined the high office. As was the custom he had written his answer in a letter presented to the Secretary of State, John Marshall.

John Marshall described what happened next: "When I waited on the President with Mr. Jay's letter declining the appointment he said thoughtfully, 'Whom shall I nominate now?' I replied that I could not tell, as I supposed that his objection to Judge Paterson remained. He said in a decided tone, 'I shall not nominate him.' After a moment's hesitation he said, 'I believe I must nominate you.' I had never before heard myself named for the office and had not even thought of it. I was pleased as well as surprised, and bowed in silence."

Marshall
Joins the Court

On January 27, 1801, the Senate gave its consent and on February 4, Marshall without hesitation accepted and took his center seat on the high bench, opening the Court for the first time in the new capital on the Potomac. Since there were only two weeks left of the Adams administration he kept his office as Secretary of State with no salary.

John Marshall

John Marshall looked older than his forty-five years. He was a tall, lean man with a dark complexion and eyes that often flashed with kindliness. Although having risen to high political office, he was still a product of frontier upbring-

John Marshall, U.S. Chief Justice for thirty-four
years (1801–35), whose grasp of legal principles
established the position of the Supreme Court.
Culver Pictures, Inc.

ing. He was pictured by one of his contemporaries as "tall, meagre, emaciated, inelegant in dress, attitudes and gesture." He was so unkempt-looking that strangers in taverns where he stopped, probably after carrying his own food home from market, mistook him for a loafer. A young, rich man one day tossed him a quarter to carry a live turkey from market and was shocked when he found out the laughing, accommodating person he hired was the Chief Justice of the United States.

Although inelegant in appearance, John Marshall had an exceptional mind. William Wirt who lived at the time described it by stating that the Chief Justice "had one original . . . almost supernatural faculty, that of developing a subject by a single glance of his mind. Nor does the exercise of it seem to cost him an effort."

John Marshall was to serve on the Supreme Court for the next thirty-four years—writing 519 of the 1106 opinions handed down by the Court. He delivered 36 of the 62 decisions involving major constitutional questions.

When he himself argued his first case before the United States Supreme Court in *Ware* versus *Hylton*, one respected eyewitness named Rufus King lauded Marshall's mind "as one of the best organized of anyone that I have known."

The Midnight Judges

One would think that not much could happen to
a Secretary of State with only two weeks left in office. John Marshall had not counted on what was
to follow. As we have seen, his earlier request to
reform the duties of the Supreme Court, particularly the arduous task of circuit riding for its
members, had been heeded. On February 13,
1801, the outgoing Federalist Congress passed
the Circuit Court Act, which relieved the Justices of circuit-riding duty. It established six new
circuit courts, requiring the appointment of six-
teen circuit judges, as well as several new district
courts. President Adams promptly filled these
positions with conservative Federalist choices.

The Organic Act
of the
District of Columbia

But the increase of judgeships did not stop. One
week exactly before the end of Adams' term, on
February 27, the Organic Act of the District of
Columbia was passed. This act authorized the
President to name justices of the peace for the

District. Adams named forty-two loyal members of his party to these offices on March 2, 1801. Confirmation came on the very next day—Adams' last day in office.

President Adams signed the documents awarding the positions to his choices. Part of John Marshall's role as Secretary of State was to affix the Great Seal of the United States to the papers for each individual justice and deliver the commission. He worked well after eight o'clock in the evening of March 3, affixing the seals. He finally gave up that evening, leaving twelve sealed but undelivered commissions. Marshall did not complete his task for the ironic reason that he was scheduled to administer the oath of office to Thomas Jefferson the following day. He was hopeful the new administration would do its duty and deliver the commissions to the appointees. Little did Marshall realize how the undelivered commissions were to affect his and the country's future.

The Marshall Court

When John Marshall's appointment as Chief Justice of the United States Supreme Court was confirmed by the Senate, he had written to President Adams, "I shall enter immediately into the duties of the office, and hope never to give you occasion to regret having made the appointment." A twenty-two foot committee room in the basement of the Capitol Building was where the new Chief Justice and five other justices who made up the Court began their first half of the August term in 1801.

Although there was only one case in the August term—*Talbot* versus *Seeman*—John Marshall immediately began to reform the past procedure of the Court. Up to this time it was not taken seriously as the coequal third branch of government along with Congress and the Presidency.

John Marshall decided that when the Court made a decision it should be issued by only one single justice—preferably the Chief Justice—for the entire court. In the past, each justice had written a separate opinion and the ruling was made by majority vote. This procedure was at times confusing and occasionally produced contradictory reasoning. Even though the vote stood, the legal profession was left puzzled and unsure of the law. Marshall changed this during his thirty-four years on the Court; he alone wrote most of the important decisions. He did talk matters over with the other justices, who could agree or dissent, but a majority agreed upon a decision that was expressed in one clear voice. The Court was seeking a moral force as great as that of Congress and the Presidency.

The very first to comment on this practice was Marshall's political enemy—Thomas Jefferson, the new President. He wrote about the new practice. "Another most condemnable practice of the Supreme Court to be corrected," he stated, "is that of cooking a decision . . . and delivering it by one of their members as the opinion of the court, without the possibility of our knowing how many, who, and for what reasons each member concurred."

Jefferson had already begun removing Adams' appointees as officers of the Court and had begun replacing them with Democratic-Republicans. But he was also looking for ways to gain control of the court system on a larger scale. During his first two years of office, his administration impeached seven judges in the lower courts.

William Marbury

In December of 1801, a situation presented itself which so outraged President Jefferson that he asked the new Congress to repeal the Judiciary Act of 1801.

During the last month of the year, an attorney, Charles Lee, came to the Supreme Court and asked that the Court help his client obtain a position of Justice of the Peace in the Washington, DC, area. His client, William Marbury, had been named in a commission signed by President Adams in the waning moments of his Presidential term. As we have seen, John Marshall, as Secretary of State, had left twelve commissions sealed but undelivered when his term ended. Marbury's commission was one of these twelve.

Charles Lee speculated that when the new Secretary of State, James Madison, took office he burned the undelivered commissions in the fireplace of his State Department office. More than likely, he did it under orders from Jefferson who felt that the District of Columbia had enough justices—but also it was a method of blocking more last-ditch Federalists from invading the court system.

Writ of Mandamus

Lee realized that the Judiciary Act of 1789 empowered the Supreme Court to issue a writ of mandamus—that is, a court order demanding an officer of the government, namely James Madison, to fulfill his duty and deliver his client's commission.

William Marbury, Lee's client, was a wealthy man and really did not need this position of Justice of the Peace. The position, which was soon to expire, also paid very little. In spite of these facts John Marshall sent the Secretary of State a bold message. Show cause, the message said, as to why a mandamus should not be sent to you requesting the deliverance of this Justice of the Peace commission. The move electrified all of Washington. President Jefferson was infuriated, especially when he heard that John Marshall had the court clerk put the case—*Marbury* versus *Madison*—on the docket or the court calendar. The case was scheduled to be presented at the Court's next term.

Jefferson Counters

Jefferson considered the show-cause order an audacious move by the Chief Justice. He considered it a direct challenge to his Presidential authority. He counter-challenged the show-cause order by ordering the new Democratic-Republican majority in Congress to intimidate the United States Supreme Court. Congress did this by eliminating the new circuit court positions, thus obligating the Supreme Court justices to ride the much-hated circuit duty again. The new Congress also abolished the High Court's June and December meeting and announced a fourteen-month recess for the court. This second move was made to insure that the Marshall Court would not immediately move to invalidate the repeal of the Judiciary Act of 1801. It also prevented a quick ruling in the Marbury case during an emotionally charged period.

The debates over the repealing of the Judiciary Act of 1801 in the House of Representatives and Senate added to the commotion. The controversy dug deeper into the fundamental differences between the Chief Justice and the President, as well as their followers. Questions began to surface as to the role of the different branches of the federal government. Was it the proper role of the Judicial Department to consider invalidating a law passed by Congress and signed by a President? Could Congress impede the function of the nation's highest court? Is the Executive Office answerable to anyone?

These were all legitimate questions that transcended party politics. Jefferson believed the Supreme Court could nullify a law, but he also believed the executive branch had the necessary

Thomas Jefferson, third president of the United States (1801–9), whose opposition to the Supreme Court inadvertently led to its increased authority. The Bettman Archive.

authority to impeach any judge who did so. It was up to the people, he claimed, ultimately to endorse the correct action through the ballot box. In the meantime, the President could execute the questionable law as though the Court had not spoken, according to Jefferson.

This was nothing more than a form of anarchy to John Marshall, and it strengthened his resolve to create "an independent judiciary" to overcome the impending chaos he foresaw.

Marshall's Dilemma

In the meantime the political warring continued. At first Marshall was tempted to disobey Congress concerning the orders to go back to the exhausting circuit-riding. But when he privately asked the other justices, he received mixed support. He, therefore, accepted the fact that he would spend the fall of 1802 riding circuit from Richmond, Virginia, to North Carolina. He waited as the months passed.

President Jefferson was relentless in attacking the judicial branch, "the last stronghold of the Federalists," by sending a message to Congress asking it to look into the conduct of Federal District Judge John Pickering of New Hampshire.

This was just five days before the session of the Supreme Court was to open on the second Monday in February 1803. Rumors abounded in Washington that Jefferson was also planning to strike at Marshall's own Court—first to try to impeach Justice Samuel Chase and if successful perhaps John Marshall himself.

Jefferson's retaliatory moves did not deter the Chief Justice from considering the case of *Marbury* versus *Madison* before the Supreme Court. The Democratic-Republicans were overjoyed that Marshall chose to take the case. To them it looked like a no-win situation for the Federalists and Marshall. If he ruled in Marbury's favor and ordered a writ of mandamus, Madison would not deliver the commission and the Court would be made to look weak and lacking any force. If he rejected Marbury's plea for the writ, it would look cowardly. Also, inaction—letting the case run out since Marbury's commission had only a bare few months to run before it terminated—would make the Court look timid and frightened. But Marshall knew the case actually represented an opportunity to establish an independent judiciary and not have the Executive Office become a law unto itself—not subject to judicial restraint.

Marbury versus Madison

On the second Monday in February 1803, Marshall had the clerk call the case of *Marbury* versus *Madison*. The administration was so confident of winning it did not even dignify the proceedings by having James Madison in attendance when the case began.

Charles Lee, William Marbury's lawyer, knew that he must prove that President Adams signed the commission for his client; otherwise it would not be valid—and no job would actually exist. He realized that John Marshall himself saw President Adams' signature on the commission but obviously, as the Chief Justice in the case, could not testify. Lee's first witness was Jacob Wagner, a clerk who worked in the office of the Secretary of State. This witness claimed he heard that Mr. Marbury's commission had been filled in and signed by the President. But when pressed to acknowledge his source of information he was too afraid to say.

Charles Lee then questioned Mr. Brent, another clerk, who testified he personally carried various commissions for Justices of the Peace to the new President's house and delivered them to Mr. Shaw, the President's aide. He added that these same commissions were returned by messenger to the office of the Secretary of State. He stated that at best, he was fairly sure Marbury's commission was among them. This was not conclusive enough for Lee and his case.

Charles Lee then called Attorney General Levi Lincoln to the stand. Lee knew that during the first two weeks of the Jefferson administration James Madison was out of town and Mr. Lincoln acted as the temporary Secretary of State. He should know about the commissions and what became of them. Levi Lincoln considered his first obligation was to remain loyal to President Jefferson and also protect himself against criminal charges should he be implicated in the destruction of these commissions. He therefore pleaded the Fifth Amendment. The Fifth Amendment protects a person from giving incriminating evidence against oneself.

The Court adjourned at the end of the first day, but on the next day Lee produced the most important witness of the case. It was James Marshall, the Chief Justice's younger brother. He attested to the fact that he had been in the office of the Secretary of State and seen the signed and sealed commission.

Marshall asked if anyone wished to speak for the government. No one came forward. It was now up to the Court to make a decision.

The Decision

On February 24, 1803, the decision was announced. It took John Marshall one and one-half hours to read it. The decision was written in the same simple style Marshall was to use for 518 decisions that were to follow during the next thirty-four years he served on the court. All his decisions reflect impressive learning and an exhaustive analysis. He first established a premise, then went on to deductions and in the process destroyed any objections to them. He would then state his conclusion supported by examples and evidence. All his decisions were written with a masterly logic, and the decision of *Marbury* versus *Madison* was not an exception.

Three Basic Questions

The present motion, wrote John Marshall, is for a mandamus. However, the Chief Justice pursued a broader answer by raising three basic questions. Has the applicant (William Marbury) a right to the commission he demands? If he has a right and that right has been violated, do the laws of the country afford him a remedy, and is it a mandamus issued from the Court?

The second section of article two of the Constitution states in part: . . . "The President shall nominate . . . shall appoint ambassadors . . . and all officers of the United States. . . ." Was this commission signed by the President, and did it have the seal of the United States affixed to it by the Secretary of State? A witness so testified. Marbury indeed has the right to the commission.

Do the laws afford Mr. Marbury a remedy? Marshall answered by stating, "The government of the United States has been emphatically termed a government of laws and not men. It would certainly cease to deserve this high appellation if the laws furnish no remedy for the violation of a vested legal right."

Wrong Court

John Marshall in seeking an answer as to how to remedy the situation for Mr. Marbury found he came to the wrong court. The Constitution makes it quite clear which cases could legally be brought first to the Supreme Court. Article three, section two, of the Constitution states, "In all cases affecting ambassadors, other public ministers and consuls and those in which a state shall be party, the Supreme Court shall have original jurisdiction." The Constitution in this same section continues, "In all other cases before-mentioned, the Supreme Court shall have appellate jurisdiction . . . ," which means to hear appeals from lower courts.

Marbury did not qualify as an ambassador or other minister—his case could be appealed to the Supreme Court but could not begin there.

Section 13
Unconstitutional

And yet John Marshall realized that the basis of the suit rested on the power given to his Court to issue writs of mandamus. This power was specifically stated in section 13 of the 1789 Judiciary Act, which set up America's federal court system. He reasoned that this power should have been given to a lower area of the court system and not to the Supreme Court. In order to change or add to the Constitution one must take a more serious step of amending the Constitution, not merely passing a piece of legislation.

In this decision he wrote to that effect: "The authority, therefore, given to the Supreme Court, by the act establishing the judicial courts of the United States, to issue the writs of mandamus to public officers, appears not to be warranted by the Constitution . . . the Constitution controls any legislative act repugnant to it. . . ." Marshall concluded that the Constitution is a superior and paramount law, unchangeable by ordinary legislative acts. Therefore any legislative act contrary to the Constitution is not a law. He added that "it is emphatically the province and the duty of the judicial department to say what the law is. . . ."

More directly he stated about the law authorizing him to issue the writ of mandamus: ". . . that a law repugnant to the Constitution is void, and that the courts, as well as the other departments are bound by that instrument." He declared section 13 of the Judiciary Act of 1789 unconstitutional.

Aftermath
of the Decision

Everyone in Washington thought John Marshall had gotten himself trapped by accepting this case. All were sure Marshall would rule in favor of Marbury on strictly political lines—they were both Federalists. It was anticipated that he would not reject the additional power given to the Court by the Judiciary Act of 1789. The situation looked as though John Marshall would fall flat on his face when the Jefferson administration refused to carry out the decision.

But the Chief Justice clearly turned the tables on everyone. On the surface he made it appear that the Court lost power in not using the writ of mandamus given it. Actually by his decision the Supreme Court gained more power. The Court gained enormous power to review the actions of the other two branches of government. What Marshall accomplished was the complete independence of the Court, while also lecturing and scolding Jefferson and Madison for not delivering Marbury his rightful Justice of the Peace commission. And at the same time he did not allow the executive branch the opportunity to defy the decision of his Court. Marshall was telling the Democratic-Republican Congress as well that they must stay within the bounds of the Constitution with all their future legislation.

Thomas Jefferson and his party were furious over this decision and derided Marshall's logic as "twistifications." John Randolph, a most ardent Democratic-Republican, cried in despair in reference to the Chief Justice, "All wrong, all wrong, but no man in the United States can tell why or wherein."

The warring between the executive branch and the judiciary branch did not cease with the Marbury decision. But it was clear that Jefferson's attacks were becoming more desperate and ridiculous. His unsuccessful attempt to impeach Justice Samuel Chase of the United States Supreme Court made him realize that his attacks on the judiciary should cease for they were becoming a "farce" (to use his own words).

Significance of
Marbury versus *Madison*
Decision

The significance of what John Marshall achieved through the case *Marbury* versus *Madison* is staggering. He established a precedent that has become part of constitutional government in the United States. What this Chief Justice accomplished was to give the Court the final word on a law, or on the powers of government under law, by the standards of the Constitution. Scholars call this judicial review.

All courts, federal and state, may exercise judicial review. Judicial review makes judges of these courts the guardians or official interpreters of the meaning of the Constitution. What the case of *Marbury* versus *Madison* performed was to clarify that the justices of the Supreme Court of the United States have the final say about the constitutionality of actions and laws.

There was little doubt that the Founding Fathers intended the federal courts to have authority to declare state laws unconstitutional. The Judiciary Act of 1789 gave this power to the United States Supreme Court. What was less clear was whether the Founding Fathers intended the Court to have the same power over acts of Congress or the President. John Marshall always believed the Supreme Court had this power. As a young lawyer trying to convince his state to ratify the Constitution, he summarized the need for judicial review by asking: "To what quarter will you look for protection from an infringement of the Constitution if you will not give the power to the judiciary (Supreme Court)? There is no other body that can afford such protection."

Prior to 1800 it was still not resolved as to whether the Supreme Court could exercise judicial review over acts of Congress or the President. President Washington believed, for example, that the Presidential veto was not to be used because of disagreement over policy but in order to protect the Constitution. As we have seen, President Jefferson opposed the Court's use of judicial review over the executive and legislative branches of the national government. Jefferson wanted the executive, legislative, and judicial branches all to decide for themselves what was constitutional or not.

John Marshall resolved this controversy in his decision of *Marbury* versus *Madison*. He wrote so plainly and compellingly in this landmark decision that it was clear the Constitution intended the Supreme Court to have the final say over acts of Congress or the President. He wrote in this decision very emphatically that the Constitution is the supreme law of the land. Acts contrary to the Constitution are null and void. And the courts are responsible for determining if acts violate the Constitution.

Albert Beveridge, one of Marshall's biographers, wrote: "Thus by a coup as bold in design and as daring in execution as that by which the Constitution had been framed, John Marshall set up a landmark in American history so high that all the future could take bearings from it."

These words have proved to be prophetic. Since *Marbury* versus *Madison* in 1803 the Supreme Court has declared all or part of more than 100 Congressional acts unconstitutional. The use of judicial review gives the United States Supreme Court a role in shaping national public policy.

Judicial review was used in critiquing Presidential actions during the Civil War. The Chief Justice Roger Taney, sitting as a federal circuit judge in the case Ex Parte Merryman in 1861, ruled that President Lincoln exceeded his executive powers in denying a person accused of treason a speedy trial in a civil court.

State actions have also been scrutinized by the nation's highest court under the power of judicial review. One such example was in the decision *Roe* versus *Wade* in 1973 whereby the majority of justices struck down laws that made performing abortion a crime.

Judicial review has been used in reviewing Congressional acts such as in *California* versus *Goldfarb* in 1977. In this case the Court ruled that certain provisions of the Social Security Act were not unconstitutional even though they did not apply equally to men and women, due to the difference in life expectancy.

John Marshall seemed to deny the United States Supreme Court additional power in the Marbury case. In refusing to permit the Court the miniscule power of issuing a writ of mandamus he gained for the court the grand power of judicial review. In doing so he established the judiciary as an independent and important branch of government; a guardian of constitutional law, as well as our rights and liberties. By making the Supreme Court the "conscience of the Constitution," John Marshall helped more than anyone else to make it a "living document."

II

THE
DRED SCOTT
DECISION

The Cotton Gin

By 1780 the increasing demand of the British mills for cotton persuaded the American farmer to give its cultivation a try. Before this time Americans had not taken cotton growing seriously. Egypt, India and the East Indies were able to meet most of the world's demand for this crop.

Green-seed or upland cotton was tried and flourished in parts of the American south. But the cotton was not profitable because the seeds could not be easily separated from the lint. It took a man working all day to clean a pound of cotton.

In 1793 Eli Whitney, a Yale graduate from Massachusetts, was staying as a tutor at Mulberry Grove, the plantation of the widow of General Nathanael Greene near Savannah, Georgia. Whitney had never seen a cotton plant before. He wrote to his father that "there were a number of very respectable gentlemen at Mrs. Greene's who all agreed that if a machine could be invented which would clean cotton with expedition, it would be a great thing both to the country and to the inventor."

He thought about the problem for a few days and then "struck out a plan of a machine." His gin (engine), which took him about ten days to design, consisted of a roller containing metal teeth. It caught a boll of cotton and pulled it through a wire mesh, leaving the seeds on the other side. The cotton lint was removed from the roller by a brush revolving against the roller. This cotton lint was later spun into cotton thread.

Eli Whitney's machine was to revolutionize the growing of cotton. With one of these "simple contrivances" a slave could clean fifty times as much cotton as by hand. The machines were easy to construct and soon larger models appeared driven by mules and horses.

White Gold

It did not take long for cotton to become a dominant southern crop, far surpassing tobacco, rice, and sugar. An average bale of cotton weighed about 500 pounds. In 1790 about 3,000 bales of the crop were produced in the United States. By the 1820s annual production hit almost one-half-million bales.

Prices for cotton also remained relatively high in spite of the avalanche of the "white gold" as the southerners called it. Fifty dollars an acre was not an unusual profit. And cotton would grow anywhere there were 200 days without frost and 24 inches of rain. It soon spread throughout Georgia and South Carolina, and after 1812 the rich central area of Alabama and northern Mississippi were taken over by this white fiber. By the 1840s cotton exports reached over the one million bale mark, a full 51 percent of America's exports.

One economist explained that for a generation beginning about 1815 cotton "was the major expansive force in the economy. The demands for the western foodstuffs and northeastern services and manufacturers were basically dependent upon income received from the cotton trade."

Even the most industrial nation of the world at the time was tied up in American southern cotton threads. England's single most important manufacture was cotton cloth. One-fifth of her nation's livelihood depended on it. And 80 percent of England's supply of cotton came from American plantations. This economic dependence both on a national and on an international level gave the South a heady sense of power. Cotton was truly king!

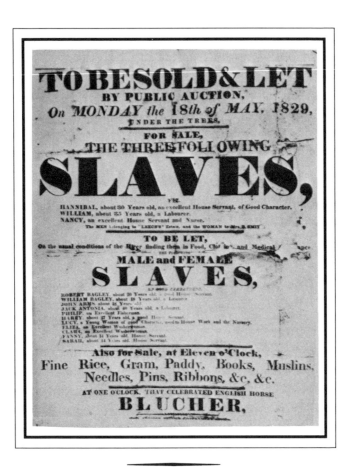

A notice advertising the sale of slaves.

The Ugly Side
of Cotton Growing

Southerners never mentioned slavery by name. Instead they called it the peculiar institution. Slaves were called the "hands" or "servants." As the profits from cotton-raising increased, so did the southern defense of slavery. Many southern slave owners rationalized that slaves lived more healthily and happily than workmen in northern factories. Planters added that northerners were really trying to hide their guilt for bringing the slaves to America in the first place.

But slave auctions presented a picture of some of the grim realities of this peculiar institution. Open selling of human flesh, sometimes along with horses and cattle, was a brutal sight. Families were separated—children taken from parents; husbands from wives; sisters from brothers. Often separations were also the result of property settlements. When the master died, frequently his "property" was divided. Slaves were treated as just that—property.

Frederick Douglass, a slave who ran away and later became a distinguished leader in the North, addressed the plight of the bondsmen. He stated that "the slave is a human being stripped of all rights—reduced to the level of a brute—a mere 'chattel.' . . . In law, the slave has no wife, no children, no country, no home. He can own nothing, acquire nothing, but must belong to another. To eat the fruit of his own toil, to clothe his person with the work of his own hands, is considered stealing . . . he labors in chains at home, under a burning sun and biting lash, so that another may ride in ease and splendor."

The Southern
Way of Life

It became increasingly clear to southerners that, as the years of the nineteenth century passed, their way of life was becoming much different from those of the free states. They needed to cling desperately to the present, woefully afraid of any criticism or change. Southern life was modeled on the aristocratic style of Western Europe. The planters lived in tall-columned and white-painted mansions. Their money provided leisure for study, reflection and public service particularly as southern statesmen. Their children were educated in the finest schools. In short, they developed their own southern gentry

A slave family on the auction block in
Charleston, SC, an engraving of 1861. The
Bettman Archive.

or southern way of life, which they were to protect with their lives.

It was becoming apparent that the southerners were forming a separate nation within the United States. John C. Calhoun, one of the leading southern statesmen, was quick to observe this impending crisis. He stated that it was "difficult to see how two people as different and as hostile [as opposed as southerners and northerners were] can exist together in one common union."

Early
Abolition Movement

The political pot began to simmer in America over the slavery question during the last term of President Andrew Jackson. This was due in no small part to the beginning of the abolitionist or antislavery agitation at this same time.

Most of the abolitionists demanded the immediate freeing of the slaves, without compensation to their masters. In their minds slavery violated the democracy expressed in the Declaration of Independence—the equality of all men. They further argued that this peculiar institution was morally wrong, was cruel and inhumane, and degraded the slave owners as well as the slaves.

William Lloyd Garrison of Massachusetts was one of the early and eloquent abolitionists. He was unyielding in his opposition to slavery. He openly burned a copy of the Constitution because it permitted such human bondage. "An agreement with hell," he called it. In 1831 his newly established newspaper *The Liberator* announced his beliefs in its first issue. "I will not equivocate, I will not excuse—I will not retreat a single inch—and I will be heard." Others who joined the movement published newspapers and held public meetings to sway public opinion.

Dred Scott

St. Louis, Missouri, was considered the gateway to the West and attracted many Americans. Among those who came in 1830 were Peter Blow and his wife, along with their three daughters, four sons, and six slaves. Mr. Blow once owned many acres of land in Virginia. He then moved to Alabama where he tried farming. He then gave up the planter's life and set up a boardinghouse called the "Jefferson Hotel" in St. Louis.

One of the six slaves had been with the Blows since birth. For his first thirty years he was raised with the Blow children and performed menial labor as a household slave. He was called Sam.

Historians are divided, but it seems likely that this slave lived more than half of his life as "Sam" and then somehow acquired the new name of Dred Scott when he was resold. Little is known of "Sam." He was probably born in Southampton County, Virginia, around the year 1795. He had very dark skin and may have been no more than five feet tall. A newspaper article published in 1857 described him as "illiterate but not ignorant," with a "strong common sense," which probably developed from his travels.

Eventually the Blow family came upon hard times. Peter Blow gave up his hotel-keeping business. His wife died in the summer of 1831 and his own health began to fail and he died the next year. In order to meet the creditors' claims against his estate, census records in 1833 show that a slave named Sam was sold for $500 to a Dr. John Emerson of St. Louis.

Dr. John Emerson

Dr. Emerson had pursued a military career and received a commission. The year after he bought Dred Scott, as Sam was now known, Dr. Emerson was assigned to Fort Armstrong in Illinois as an assistant surgeon. He was then transferred to

Dred Scott, whose suit for his freedom reached
the Supreme Court. The Bettman Archive.

Fort Snelling in the Wisconsin Territory, near the present-day St. Paul, Minnesota. Scott accompanied his master in both places until 1842. Slavery was prohibited in Illinois by that state's constitution and in the northern part of the Louisiana Purchase by the Compromise of 1820.

While in the service of Emerson, Scott received permission to marry Harriet Robinson, whose master transferred ownership of her to the doctor. Dred and Harriet Scott had two daughters: Eliza born in 1838 and Lizzie born about 1845. Dr. Emerson himself married Eliza Irene Sanford on February 6, 1838. It was her brother, John F. A. Sanford, who played a large role in the historic Dred Scott court case.

The Minnesota winters were too hard for Dr. Emerson, and his request for a transfer was honored. He was sent to Fort Jessup, Louisiana. The damp climate there also bothered the doctor. In his letter to the army seeking yet another change, back to Fort Snelling in St. Louis, he listed some of the difficulties he was having. It included the fact that "even one of my negroes . . . has sued for freedom." No record was ever found of this suit. Historians are not sure whether Dred Scott might have been that slave.

The army again accommodated the request for transfer and the Emersons and Scotts arrived back at Fort Snelling in St. Louis on September 21, 1838. Dred Scott had been taken not just once but twice into free areas. In the spring of 1840 the doctor received orders to go to Florida where American military forces were fighting against Seminole Indians. He left his wife and slaves in St. Louis with Mrs. Emerson's father. The doctor returned in 1843 and died that same year.

It is unclear what happened to the Scotts during the next three years, but it seems likely that they were hired out to various people. In 1846 a few weeks after they were hired to a man named Samuel Russell, Dred Scott and his family sued for their freedom. They claimed they had lived in a free state and a free territory and were therefore free.

The Suit

There is a mystery that surrounds the suit. Why had Scott waited so long to bring it? He had been eligible in free territory since 1834. Perhaps he was unaware of the law. Who informed him and why? Historians claim that the motives of the people involved were straightforward and personal. They did not set out to create a test case. People familiar with the Missouri law knew Scott

Harriet Scott, who joined her husband in his
legal battle for freedom.

had a strong case. The highest court had ruled time and time again that a master who took his slave to reside in a territory or state where slavery was outlawed had to set him free. Perhaps Dred Scott initiated his own case with the help of friends.

The record shows that on April 6, 1846, Francis Butter Murdock, an abolitionist lawyer, posted the necessary bonds and filed the required papers. Perhaps the black pastor Reverend John R. Anderson of the Second African Baptist Church in St. Louis helped. Harriet Scott was a member of the congregation. These people may have initiated the suit, but it is clear that Taylor Blow, son of Scott's original owners, carried the suit out to the very end. He stepped in with the necessary financial aid after Francis Murdock left the scene two months after bringing the case to court. It would be eleven long years of litigation before a final decision in the case was rendered by the United States Supreme Court.

Scott Wins

One of St. Louis' historic remnants today, the "Old Courthouse," was new and unfinished in 1847. It was the site of the initial engagement in

Dred Scott's legal battle for freedom. He was represented by Samuel M. Boy the former attorney-general of Missouri. All that needed to be proven was that Scott had been taken to a free territory and was now claimed by Mrs. Emerson, the doctor's widow, as a slave. The first point was easily established. But because of a technicality, a new trial had to be declared. It was not until January 12, 1850, that the case finally came to retrial.

In the meantime Mrs. Emerson's father died, and she left St. Louis to live with one of her sisters in Springfield, Massachusetts. John Sanford then took over his sister's affairs and hired a new set of lawyers for the retrial. The jury found in favor of Dred Scott. He was momentarily a free man!

But the Sanford forces were not to give up that easily. They appealed the case to the state supreme court. The necessary briefs were filed in 1850. And again because of some error of detail in the procedure, the state's highest court did not rule until 1852.

National Discord

In the meantime the public feeling in the slave-holding states was becoming more hostile toward freedom-seeking suits. This change of attitude coincided with the rising temperature of the sectional conflict. In 1845 just before leaving office President John Tyler suggested that Congress admit Texas into the union. Northerners feared such an annexation would open up more territory to slavery and increase southern representation in the House of Representatives. It might even increase southern membership in the Senate should such a large area be subdivided into several states.

The newly elected President in 1845 was James K. Polk. He ran on an expansionist platform, and part of it called for the reannexation of Texas. Many Americans believed the area of Texas was part of the original Louisiana Purchase in 1803. Mexico did not appreciate America's expansionist appetite and particularly her support of the successful Texan War for independence in 1845. Mexican-American relations became further strained when Texas was admitted into the Union on December 29, 1845. This admission led the way to the Mexican-American

War the following year. In this war the United States easily defeated Mexico in 1848.

But it was the conquest of some 500,000 square miles of territory, which Mexico was forced to cede to the United States, that inflamed the already dangerous quarrel between the slavery and free-soil forces in Congress. Also in 1848, gold was discovered in California, a part of the Mexican Cession. It was not long before 100,000 people occupied this Pacific Coast area and they wished to enter the Union as a free state, free of slavery. The north-south sectional quarrel over the question of slavery became intensified. Americans again faced the question of the status of slavery in newly acquired territory.

Fortunately, Henry Clay of Kentucky, known as "the Great Compromiser," proposed a solution. California was to be admitted as a free state. The rest of the Mexican Cession was divided into the territories of New Mexico and Utah; they were to follow the principle of popular sovereignty. This rule permitted territorial inhabitants to decide whether or not they wanted slavery. Slave trade, but not slavery, was prohibited in the nation's capital. A stricter fugitive slave law was also stipulated.

Senator Daniel Webster of Massachusetts helped Clay get this "Compromise of 1850" passed in the Senate. He had to beat back the antislavery forces as well as southern opposition. Calhoun remained the southern spokesman and although dying he had a fellow Senator read his speech. He warned the North to stop interfering with slavery; otherwise, "let the states . . . part in peace."

The Temporary Lull

The Compromise of 1850 provided a temporary lull in the conflict over slavery. America was drifting toward disunion. This movement was being reflected in Presidential politics. In the election of 1848 both the Democratic and the Whig parties sat on the lid of the slavery-issue cauldron. They both tried to ignore the boiling within. Much of the reality was reflected by the formation of a strong third party—the Free Soil Party. This political party opposed the extension of slavery in the territories.

The Presidential election of 1852 witnessed the hopeless split of the Whig Party—its northern and southern wings unable to agree on the Fugitive Slave Law. After winning two Presidential races in 1840 and 1848 the Whig Party disintegrated and became one of the first major casualties of the fiery slave issue.

Sectional tensions became further strained when in 1852 Harriet Beecher Stowe produced the novel, *Uncle Tom's Cabin*. Several hundred thousand copies were sold in its first year. The book portrayed the wickedness and evil of slavery. Stowe's work made a lasting impression on the North, and many of its readers swore from this point on they would not enforce the provisions of the Fugitive Slave Law.

Missouri Supreme Court

For the first time the controversial political beliefs growing in the country entered into the Dred Scott case. Slavery, its morality or its legality, became a public issue in Missouri politics. There had always been a long-standing rule in Missouri that once a slave was taken to free territory that slave was to be free. "Once free always free." This principle would still hold true in spite of the fact that the freed slave voluntarily decided to return to the slave state of Missouri. But now slavery was under fierce attack, and some members of the Missouri court decided to use the Scott case to defend their state's self-interest. The judges did not feel compelled to honor the laws of another state, in this case of Illinois. This judgment was especially true if the particular state's laws were hostile to slavery.

So on March 22, 1852, the Supreme Court of Missouri announced a 2 to 1 decision reversing the decision of the lower court and finding Dred Scott was still a slave.

The Federal Court Next

Scott acquired new legal counsel and by the end of 1853 filed a new suit in federal court. The lawyers were told that Irene Emerson was now the wife of Calvin C. Chafee, of Springfield, Massachusetts, and that she had recently sold the Scotts to her brother John F. A. Sanford. He resided in New York City. This situation allowed Dred Scott's lawyers the opportunity to bring suit in the Missouri federal court as a case concerning "citizens of different states." His lawyers stated that Scott was a citizen of Missouri and that Sanford was a citizen of New York. They preferred to sue in a lower federal court rather than to appeal directly to the United States Supreme Court.

The lawyers were aware of a recent Supreme Court case similar to Scott's.

The *Strader* versus *Graham* case involved slave musicians in Kentucky who were taken to the free territory of Ohio for performances. They later fled from Kentucky to Canada. The suit was not for their freedom but a demand for damages by their owner from those who helped their escape. The defense lawyers claimed that the slaves were free by virtue of the 1787 Northwest Ordinance, which banned slavery in that area. The Kentucky Court of Appeals rejected this argument and voted in favor of the slaveowners.

The case then went to the United States Supreme Court where Chief Justice Roger B. Taney, speaking for a unanimous court, dismissed the case for lack of jurisdiction. The Northwest Ordinance was no longer in effect because it had been superseded by the constitution and laws of the states. The nonruling in this case made the Kentucky Court of Appeals decision stand—the blacks were still slaves, and this case might be used against Dred Scott.

On May 13, 1854, in a plain rented upstairs room in the Pepin Building, on First Street between Chestnut and Pine in St. Louis, the case of Dred Scott versus John A. Sanford was heard. This was the federal district court in St. Louis.

Scott was asserting that he was a citizen of Missouri and that his wife and two children were wrongfully imprisoned. He claimed $9,000 in damages.

Sanford's lawyers pleaded that there should be no trial—since Scott was Negro of African descent, he could claim no citizenship of the United States. Noncitizens were not permitted to sue in federal court. Federal Judge Robert Wells denied this plea of Sanford's lawyers. He claimed anyone who had legal capacity to own property and lived in a state was a citizen. This federal judge considered Dred Scott a citizen.

The trial then proceeded and the jury ruled in favor of the defendant John A. Sanford. Dred Scott's lawyers immediately moved to appeal to the United States Supreme Court. A crowded docket prevented a hearing of *Scott* versus *Sanford* until February 1856, almost two years after the federal district court decision.

The Presidential Election

In the election of 1856 the Democrats, wishing to straddle the fence on the slavery issue, nominated James Buchanan, a Pennsylvanian with southern sympathies. The new Republican Party

A caricature of President James Buchanan at the
time of the Dred Scott decision.

selected the famous western explorer, John C. Fremont. He was opposed to slavery. Despite the Republican's catchy slogan, "Free Soil, Free men, Fremont and victory," Buchanan won handily. It must be noted that the newly created Republican Party made quite an impressive first showing in a Presidential race.

One month before Buchanan's inauguration on February 7, 1856, the Supreme Court was nearly ready to hear the case of *Scott* versus *Sanford*. The case had received very little advance publicity in newspapers across America. The highly volatile national political issues in this case had not yet attracted public attention.

But to President-Elect Buchanan this case seemed a way to settle the slavery issue once and for all. He wanted the United States Supreme Court to decide that slavery could be extended to all United States territory, and he took an unprecedented step to see that it did so. By meddling in the affairs of the Supreme Court he ignored the traditional separation of the three branches of government.

The Taney Court

The case initially seemed to take a routine path. The Supreme Court justices heard the arguments from the opposing lawyers in May 1856. The majority of the justices seemed to wish to dispose of the case by upholding the decision of the lower court. Most felt Dred Scott was not free, and they would defend their decision by referring to the *Strader* versus *Graham* case.

But then the political makeup of the Court itself began to show and become a major factor in the decision-making process. John McLean, a former Congressman and United States Postmaster General, was the only Republican on the Court. He was from the state of Ohio. Benjamin R. Curtis belonged to the Whig Party and came from Massachusetts. The remaining seven justices on the Court were all Democrats; five were southerners and two came from northern states. Robert C. Grier came from Pennsylvania, and Samuel Nelson was a New Yorker. The justices representing the slave states included: Chief Justice Taney, from Maryland; Justice James M. Wayne of Georgia; John Catron of Tennessee; Peter V. Daniel a native of Virginia; and John A. Campbell of Alabama.

It seemed that "Potomac fever" reached one of the justices. He was thinking of using the decision to strengthen his chances of being nominated in the Presidential race of 1860. Justice John McLean of Ohio announced he was going to write a dissent to the case declaring Scott a free man and also support the idea that Congress had the right to ban slavery in the territories. McLean had been a strong contender for the Republican nomination in the 1856 Presidential race but lost out to Fremont at the Republican convention. Justice Curtis claimed he would dissent as well.

The Court then thought it wise to postpone a decision until after the 1856 election. Because of the prolonged illness of Justice Daniel, the Court did not hold its first conference on the case until February 14, 1856. At this point it seemed that only five of the nine justices wished to rule on the broad question of whether Congress had the right to ban slavery in the territories. With such a thin majority and on strictly sectional lines that part of the decision was dropped.

Justice Nelson was assigned to write the majority decision upholding the lower court's decision in which six other justices were to concur. Nelson produced a short opinion of about five thousand words. The ink was not dry on this ma-

Justice John McLean, from Ohio, the only
Republican on the court and one of two
dissenting justices declaring Scott a free man.
The Supreme Court Historical Society.

jority opinion when suddenly the Court changed its approach.

Buchanan Influence

There was pressure from many quarters to broaden the question taken up by the High Court. Proslavery Congressmen kept badgering the members of the Supreme Court. They were trying to get the southern majority to hand down a decision protecting slavery. These proponents of slavery argued that here was an opportunity by acting boldly to dispose of a dangerous public issue. Some of the southern justices on the Court had the chance now to help the South fight the insulting laws that intruded on their way of life. Some of this pressure seemed to work especially on Georgian Justice James Wayne. He seems to have been chiefly responsible for the Court's decision to take up the broader issue.

In the meantime President-Elect James Buchanan was hoping for a decision by the Court that would limit the power of Congress over the slavery question. He took the unusual step of writing his friend Justice John Catron on the Court asking whether a decision would be made before his March 4 Inauguration date. He wished to make a statement about the question of slavery in his address. Catron replied that the decision would be made in February but "would not help" because the question of Congress' role in regard to slavery would not be addressed.

At the same time Justice Wayne persuaded Chief Justice Taney and the other southern justices to do just that: address the larger question of the legality of the Missouri Compromise. It would be helpful if one northern judge also agreed. So to this end Justice Catron wrote back to Buchanan asking him to use his influence on Justice Grier of Pennsylvania.

The President wrote Grier and received an imprudent and extraordinary reply. This unique communication gives great insight into what transpired during this case in the secret chambers of America's highest Court. Grier stated: "We fully appreciate and concur in your views as to the desirableness at this time of having an expression from the Court on this troublesome question. It appeared that our brothers who dissented from the majority [to uphold the lower federal court's decision] especially Justice McLean, were determined to come out with a long and labored dissent. . . ." But now, Grier pointed out to the President, there was a reversal of the original limited approach to the legal question.

Justice Robert C. Grier, from Pennsylvania,
whose letter to President Buchanan concerning
the Dred Scott case breached the traditional
separation of the judicial and executive
branches of government. The Supreme Court
Historical Society.

And "there will therefore be six, if not seven (perhaps Nelson will remain neutral) who will decide the Compromise Law of 1820 to be of non-effect. [This is the law that banned slavery in the Louisiana Purchase area above the 36° 30′ parallel.] But the opinions will not be delivered before Friday the 16th of March. . . . We thought it due to you to state to you in candor and confidence the real state of the matter."

So Buchanan with this inside information seemed fair-minded about the question of slavery in his March 4 Inaugural Address. He declared the question "is a judicial question which legitimately belongs to the Supreme Court of the United States before whom it is now pending. . . . To their decision in common with all good citizens, I shall cheerfully submit, whatever it might be."

Chief Justice Taney
Delivers the Decision

At this point a great deal of interest had developed over the impending decision. A Supreme Court courtroom is usually sparsely attended. But on this chilly Friday morning of March 6,

1857, the courtroom located in the basement of the Capitol Building was jammed with journalists and spectators.

Dred Scott was not present. He was at home in St. Louis living as a hired-out slave. John F. A. Sanford was in an insane asylum and would be dead within two months. Both of these litigants seemed insignificant to the case. Events had dictated the direction the case would take—it was no longer the simple point of "once free always free" at issue. When Scott went to court back in 1846, the principle was universally accepted that once a slave touched free territory, he or she was free. That basic idea was about to be abandoned.

Chief Justice Taney began reading the decision at 11:00 o'clock to a tense audience. Many were hopeful that the judicial branch could come up with an answer to the slavery controversy, taking on the responsibility from a deadlocked Congress and an executive branch with a freshman incumbent as President.

The Chief Justice, now almost 80 years old, spoke in a soft low voice for almost two hours. His voice steadily weakened as the hours wore on. Justices Samuel Nelson and John Catron followed with shorter opinions. Justice McLean and Curtis, the dissenters, spoke the next day. They took up five hours of time.

Roger B. Taney, U.S. Chief Justice for twenty-eight years (1836–64), whose most famous decision was in the Dred Scott case. The Bettman Archive.

When all were finished what was crystal clear was that by a vote of 7 to 2 Dred Scott and his family were still slaves and not free citizens.

The Question of Citizenship

Of the fifty-five pages of Taney's opinion almost half were spent on the issue of Negro citizenship. For Judge Wells at the lower federal court level it had been a simple matter. Any resident capable of owning property was a citizen. Not for Taney—he claimed Negroes were not citizens at the time of the writing of the Declaration of Independence and the Constitution. Dred Scott was not a citizen of Missouri or any other state. Blacks, he claimed, ". . . had for more than a century been regarded as being of an inferior race, either in social or political relations; and so far inferior, that they had no rights which the white man was bound to respect. . . ."

Scott was not entitled, therefore, to sue Sanford in federal court because he was not a citizen within the meaning of the Constitution of the United States. Justice Taney had shifted the focus from a person being a citizen based on state qualifications to federal qualifications. He changed the original question of whether Scott was a citizen of the state of Missouri to one of whether he was a citizen of the United States. And he made the right to sue in federal court dependent on a person enjoying all rights under the federal Constitution. Judge Wells according to Taney had been in error in accepting the case in his court.

At this point, the Chief Justice's critics claim, he should have remanded (sent back) the case to the lower court with instructions to dismiss for want of jurisdiction. Instead he argued that he was offering additional reasons for dismissal on jurisdictional grounds. So he proceeded to address the question of whether Dred Scott had become free by virtue of his living in Illinois or at Fort Snelling.

The Missouri Compromise Unconstitutional

Taney went on to claim that Scott would not be a free man even though he lived in free territory. This, the Chief Justice claimed, was so because the Fifth Amendment states that no person may be deprived of his property without due process of law. A slave was treated similarly in law to a person's house, horse, or handbag. Thus, the Fifth Amendment protected the slaveowner from having anyone take away his personal property. Congress had gone beyond its authority when it passed the Missouri Compromise in 1820, forbidding or abolishing slavery in the territories. Having a slaveowner run the risk of losing his property if, for example, he chose to take the slave-property to Wisconsin was against the Constitution. Therefore, the Missouri Compromise was unconstitutional. Congress was not allowed to ban slavery in the territories, and it followed that neither could any of the territorial legislatures.

In addition, Justice Taney's opinion made the point that Scott was a slave because his status was determined by the state he was from and not the state he was taken to. Missouri courts ruled him a slave—that was the governing factor. "Once free always free" no longer existed.

Taney's decision was accepted as "the decision" of the Court but there were varying points of agreement and disagreement in the majority position. All seven justices agreed that Scott was a slave and the laws of Missouri determined his status. Six of the justices believed the Missouri

Compromise was unconstitutional, and only three maintained that a Negro could not be a citizen.

Justices Curtis and McLean in disagreeing with the majority opinion claimed Scott was a citizen and free. They both agreed that the Missouri Compromise was constitutional. Curtis felt the Court should not have ruled on the constitutionality of the Compromise after it had declared Scott had no right to sue in federal court. It therefore followed, he added, that the majority opinion was not binding on anybody.

Reaction to the Decision

The Dred Scott decision sent shock waves through the nation. The antislavery forces had a head start in their criticism. The opinions of the dissent came out quite a while before Taney's majority opinion. Justice Curtis accused the Chief Justice of rewriting his opinion in an attempt to refute the more convincing dissenting arguments.

The newspapers led the way and set the tone of criticism. Horace Greeley's *New York Tribune* rang out with a description of the decision as "atrocious," "wicked," "detestable hypocrisy." This newspaper described the Court as one that "rushed into politics, voluntarily, and without other purpose than to preserve the cause of slavery. . . ."

The *New York Evening Post* is quoted as saying: "If this decision shall stand for law the nation's flag should be dyed black, and its device should be the whip and the fetter. . . ."

One of these same northern newspapers described the decision as one that was "entitled to just as much moral weight as would be the judgement of a majority congregated in a Washington barroom."

The southern press shot back with the principle that the Court had ruled and all Americans must obey. The *Constitutionalist* of Augusta, Georgia, declared: "Southern opinion upon this subject of southern slavery . . . is now the supreme law of the land . . . and opposition to southern opinion upon this subject is now opposition to the Constitution and morally treason against the government."

The Republican Party was well aware that the Dred Scott decision struck at the very heart of their reason for political existence. The new national party's major policy centered on not allow-

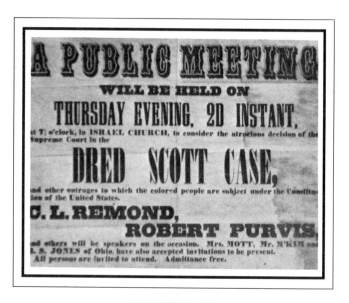

A PUBLIC MEETING

WILL BE HELD ON

THURSDAY EVENING, 2D INSTANT,

at 7, o'clock, in ISRAEL CHURCH, to consider the atrocious decision of the Supreme Court in the

DRED SCOTT CASE,

and other outrages to which the colored people are subject under the Constitution of the United States.

C. L. REMOND,
ROBERT PURVIS,

and others will be speakers on the occasion. Mrs. MOTT, Mr. M'KIM and I. S. JONES of Ohio, have also accepted invitations to be present. All persons are invited to attend. Admittance free.

Philadelphia citizens call for a protest meeting against the Dred Scott decision.

80

ing slavery to be extended into the new territories. The Court's ruling was a setback. The Republicans did, however, answer the Dred Scott decision with the accusation that Chief Justice Taney went beyond the merits of the case when he ruled on the repeal of the Missouri Compromise. *"Obiter dictum,"* the Latin term for "something said in passing," was their battlecry.

A great women's rights advocate, Susan B. Anthony, issued a comment about the Dred Scott decision that was most profound. She felt the Supreme Court was really measuring the sickness that came over the country concerning the issue of slavery. "Judge Taney's decision as infamous as it is," she said, "is but the reflection of the spirit and practice of the American people, North as well as South."

What Happened to Dred Scott

All the members of the Dred Scott family were given their freedom on May 26, 1857. Dr. Calvin C. Chafee, who had married Irene Sanford Emerson, immediately after the Supreme Court decision transferred ownership of Scott back to

Taylor Blow in St. Louis, Missouri. The Blow family formally freed Dred Scott, his wife Harriet and two daughters. The action occurred in the same courtroom in St. Louis where the case had started over ten years before. Dred Scott died on September 17, 1858, of tuberculosis.

Some Historical Perspective

In 1974 the *American Bar Association Journal* asked its readers to determine by ballot what milestones of legal history should be celebrated in a proposed Bicentennial volume. The lawyers, judges and law professors participating selected fourteen Supreme Court decisions, and Dred Scott ranked fifth among the fourteen chosen as notable landmark cases. The voting placed it right behind the *Brown* versus *Board of Education* opinion and ahead of every Marshall decision except *Marbury* versus *Madison*.

The Dred Scott decision takes on such significance because it impacted on many levels of our American history. Taney and his southern brethren on the Court "planned to defeat the abolitionists and to avoid disaster," according to Carl B. Swisher, his biographer. Instead the decision fueled and perhaps accelerated the pace toward the Civil War. This same biographer claims that Taney's statement in the Dred Scott case that blacks were inferior to whites—"that they had no rights which the white man was bound to respect"—was not a personal belief of the Chief Justice. He was saying this because he thought it was the general belief at the time at which the Constitution was written. But whether taken out of context or not this statement created a racial legacy that carried over into the twentieth century. This was a shocking and unfortunate result of the Dred Scott decision.

The Scott case in declaring that blacks both free and slave were not and could not be citizens led to the eventual passage, after the Civil War, of one of America's most important civil rights laws, the Fourteenth Amendment to the Constitution. This Amendment states that all persons born or naturalized in the United States are citizens of the United States and of the state wherein they reside. And that no state shall abridge the privileges or immunities of citizens of the United States. The question of the citizenship of blacks was forever settled!

When Chief Justice Roger Taney declared the

Missouri Compromise of 1820 unconstitutional he employed the legal precedent of judicial review for the first time at the federal level since Marshall's *Marbury* versus *Madison* decision. This historical event in our constitutional history was obscured by the avalanche of criticism this case received. Instead of immediately strengthening the concept of judicial review, the Dred Scott decision caused much of the country to temporarily lose faith in the United States Supreme Court and in the idea that this institution was the final arbiter of the Constitution.

Constitutional historian Edward S. Corwin has written about this point. He states: "When [one] finds six judges arriving at precisely the same result by three distinct processes of reasoning, he is naturally disposed to surmise that the result may possibly have induced the processes rather than the processes compelled the result. . . ."

William Cullen Bryant's *New York Evening Post* on March 14, 1857, charged the Supreme Court with "judicial impertinence" in assuming the power to "act as the interpreter of the Constitution for the other branches of government." Lincoln in 1858 claimed, "If I were in Congress and a vote should come up on a question whether slavery should be prohibited in a new territory, in spite of that Dred Scott decision, I would vote that it should." He believed that the decision would some day be overruled and in the meantime it should simply be ignored.

The erosion of the prestige of the United States Supreme Court as an important and influential national institution was perhaps the greatest impact of the Dred Scott case. Before the decision there was a willingness to look to the Court to solve difficult constitutional problems. After Dred Scott, confidence on such cases disappeared. As for the legality of slavery, it required the Civil War to settle the question.

A contemporary editorial written in the *North American Review* of October 1857 calculated the damages to the Court: "The country will feel the consequences of the decision more deeply and more permanently in the loss of confidence in sound judicial integrity and strictly legal character of their tribunals, than in anything beside; and this, perhaps, may well be accounted the greatest political calamity which this country under our forms of government, could sustain."

It would take quite a number of years for the United States Supreme Court to recover from what Chief Justice Charles Evans Hughes was later to describe as "a self-inflicted wound."

III

UNITED
STATES
VERSUS
NIXON

The Thirty-Seventh President

Reflecting on the prevalent attitude in the White House between 1969 and 1974, one Presidential aide commented: "I mean if you worked for someone he was God, and whatever the orders were, you did it." The head of this administration was Richard M. Nixon, the thirty-seventh President of the United States. The Nixon administration developed problems with unethical and unlawful actions, especially in connection with the Presidential reelection campaign in 1972. These wrongdoings became known to the American public as the Watergate scandals, and they raised some unusual constitutional questions.

Americans had faced scandal before. The Ulysses S. Grant administration had so much corruption, for example, that it was dubbed "the era of good stealing." President Harding in the 1920s had his "Teapot Dome" scandal, which dealt with misuse of government oil reserves. These scandals involved money—the Watergate affair involved the misuse of power. The transgressions in his administration when ultimately uncovered led to President Nixon's resignation—a first in American history.

The officials of this administration and their accomplices masterminded the cover-up of "hush-money" payments to burglars; the misuse of government departments such as the Central Intelligence Agency, Internal Revenue Service, and Federal Bureau of Investigation; the disruption of the campaigns of their leading Democratic opponents; the receiving of illegal reelection campaign contributions; and the illegal placement of taping devices, among a number of other things.

None of this wrongdoing appears to have been necessary in 1972. The Nixon administration seemed to be in a strong political position. In fact, the Presidential returns of that year's election found Richard Nixon receiving 60.8 percent of the popular vote and 97 percent of the electoral vote.

The Watergate
Break-In

The beginning of the downfall of this Presidency took place in the predawn hours of June 17, 1972, shortly before the Presidential nominating conventions. Alerted by the security guard, three plainclothesmen arrested five men who had broken into the Democratic National Committee headquarters. Ultimately seven suspects were rounded up, and this group became known as the Watergate Seven. The headquarters were located on the sixth floor of an office building in Watergate, a cluster of stylish apartments and offices facing the Potomac River in Washington, DC. The burglars carried two expensive cameras, 40 rolls of film, and a number of listening devices known as "bugs," as well as large sums of money in new $100 bills in their wallets. It was later learned this was a second break-in; its purpose was to repair an already placed tap on Democratic Chairman Lawrence O'Brien's telephone.

Suspicion soon fell on the Republican party because one of those apprehended was James W. McCord, Jr., an electronics expert, who was working for the Committee for the Reelection of the President (CREEP). Before the month was up the Federal Bureau of Investigation was able to track down two more Watergate conspirators. They both had even closer ties to the Nixon administration. One was G. Gordon Liddy, who worked for the same committee as McCord. The other was E. Howard Hunt, who had been working for the White House as a consultant on security matters.

The Democrats tried to profit from the Watergate burglary, announcing a one-million-dollar civil suit against the Committee for the Re-election of the President. But President Nixon denied responsibility for the actions of the Watergate Seven. "I can say categorically that no one on the White House staff," he claimed on June 22, "no one in this administration presently employed was involved in this bizarre incident." Most of the public took the President's word.

The McCord Letter

Early in 1973 the Watergate burglars were put on trial before Judge John J.Sirica, who was the chief judge of the United States District Court, in Washington, DC. Most of them pleaded guilty and this meant they could not be questioned about the case. Judge Sirica passed severe sentences on those convicted in an attempt to force one or more of them to turn state's evidence in exchange for leniency.

The first break in the wall of silence put up by the administration aides came when Judge Sirica announced that James McCord, one of the Watergate defendants, had revealed in a letter that some of the defendants had been paid "hush

John J. Sirica, the judge who presided over a number of cases involved in the Watergate affair. AP/Wide World Photos

money" to plead guilty in order to guarantee their silence. It was later proven that E. Howard Hunt, Jr., had received at least $75,000 from White House sources to secure his silence. Hunt's wife died in a Chicago plane crash on December 8, 1972, and $10,000 in cash was found in her handbag. The money was traced to secret pay-offs made to other convicted Watergate burglars. Mr. McCord also told Judge Sirica that some who testified had lied under oath and others involved in the Watergate affair were named. The judge, who suspected there was more behind the simple break-in, had already announced that a Watergate grand jury would be kept in session. It would be ready to indict any other officials should new evidence turn up. James McCord agreed to give further testimony to this grand jury and to a newly formed Senate Watergate investigating committee.

The Watergate Committee

Stirred by Judge Sirica's findings and by newspaper reports of alleged wrongdoings in the Nixon administration, the Senate appointed a special investigating committee, called a Select Committee. It was to inquire into unethical and illegal activities in connection with the 1972 election. Senator Sam Ervin of North Carolina was Chairman of this Select Committee that came to be called the Watergate Committee. Joining him on the committee were six other Senators.

In a secret session James McCord told this panel that CREEP chairman John Mitchell was the "overall boss" of the Watergate break-in. A month prior to the Watergate Committee opening its nationally televised hearings, President Nixon was informed by Assistant Attorney General Henry Peterson that his chief White House aides could possibly be indicted on charges for their role in the Watergate cover-up. This information led the President to announce on national television the resignation of his closest aides, H. R. Haldeman and John Ehrlichman as well as his counsel John Dean. The latter was already seeking immunity from prosecution in return for telling all he knew. Also, eight days after the Watergate Committee began its hearings on May 17, 1973, Elliot Richardson was sworn in as the new Attorney General replacing Richard Kleindienst.

In order to secure Senate confirmation of his appointment, Richardson agreed to establish the office of a Watergate Special Prosecutor. Archibald Cox, a Harvard professor, was appointed head of that office by President Nixon. Cox was promised full authority to prosecute cases without interference.

The Watergate Hearings

The Watergate hearings, chaired by Senator Ervin, were televised nationally and at times commanded television audiences of up to 25 million people. The task of this committee was to gather data and recommend to the full Senate legislation that would prevent future Watergates. The testimony of the witnesses before the committee caused a national furor.

High level government officials came before the Watergate Committee. They were questioned about alleged crimes and unethical practices. On occasion some of these officials confessed to wrongdoings. James McCord, one of the first witnesses, stated that it was Jack Caufield, working for CREEP, who promised him money to keep quiet and a job as well as clemency. Caufield, when questioned by the commit-

Senator Sam Ervin, Chairman of the Senate
Investigating Committee, presiding over the
Watergate hearings. AP/Wide World Photos

tee, admitted he indeed made this offer with the authorization of John Dean.

Jeb Magruder former special assistant to the President and former deputy director of CREEP confessed he had committed perjury in past testimony about Watergate. He also implicated John Mitchell and John Dean, claiming they both approved of the break-in.

The first witness to implicate President Richard Nixon was John Dean. He had a remarkable memory and he filled 245 pages of testimony openly accusing the President of complicity in the Watergate cover-up. He charged the President with saying that one million dollars was not too much for hush money. Dean spoke about Nixon's disregard for the law, his excessive concern with press leaks, as well as mentioning the fact that the President kept an "enemies list" made up of anyone who opposed him.

At this point in the Watergate hearings it was John Dean's word pitted against that of the President of the United States. But then on July 16 something unexpected occurred that would lead to the testing of the veracity of Dean's testimony.

The Senate Watergate Investigating Committee
hearings being held, May 23, 1973. Committee
members are at right. AP/Wide World Photos

Taping Revealed

Testifying before the committee in a rather matter-of-fact manner, Alexander P. Butterfield, a deputy assistant to President Nixon, revealed that the Secret Service had installed tape recorders in the White House. They were located in the Oval Office, in the Lincoln room, at Camp David, and in the Executive Office Building. They were turned on only when Nixon was present. He said Nixon authorized these devices for the purpose of keeping a historic record. All conversations of the President's guests, which included his own private staff and visiting dignitaries as well as Congressmen, were recorded without their knowledge or their permission.

Battle of the Tapes
—Part I

As soon as this startling testimony was disclosed, both the Watergate Committee and Special Prosecutor Archibald Cox asked the White House for the tapes containing discussions of the Watergate affair. Cox specifically asked for tapes of nine conversations. President Nixon refused to turn over the tapes, claiming such a request violated executive privilege—the right of a President to have confidential conversations with his aides and other officials.

The White House ignored Cox's subpoena for the tapes, and the case went before Judge Sirica. Sirica ruled that the tapes should be submitted to him, and he would then decide whether they should be given to the Special Prosecutor. President Nixon defied this ruling. The case next went to the United States Circuit Court of Appeals, which ruled that the President must give Judge Sirica the tapes.

On October 19, 1973, President Nixon made a suggestion about submitting the relevant parts of the tapes to Judge Sirica. He would do this provided the Prosecutor's office would not make any further requests for tapes. His friend Senator John Stennis would even listen to the tapes and vouch for their authenticity.

The Special Prosecutor refused this offer. The President immediately asked Elliot Richardson, the Attorney General, to fire Cox. Rather than do this, Richardson himself—and his Deputy Attorney General when also asked to fire Cox—resigned. Finally Robert Bork, the third ranking member of the Justice Department, as acting Attorney General, relieved Cox of his post.

The "Saturday Massacre," as it was to be called, created an uproar in the country. The White House was inundated with letters and telegrams demanding the President's impeachment. Some of his staunchest supporters now doubted his innocence. A week after the "Saturday Massacre" the House Judiciary Committee began considering the possible impeachment of Richard Nixon. The President at that point had to deal with three investigating bodies—the Senate Watergate Committee, the Special Watergate Prosecutor, and the House of Representatives Judiciary Committee, where the impeachment process would begin.

The White House, caught in this unexpected tidal wave of criticism and scrutiny, backed down. The President agreed to turn the tapes over to Judge Sirica with the understanding that the pertinent material would be sent to the grand jury investigating the Watergate affair and nothing would be revealed to the public. President Nixon also named a new special prosecutor, Leon Jaworski. The Texas lawyer and former American Bar Association president accepted the job on the condition he be given independence and full cooperation by the White House. However, three weeks after the appointment of Jaworski, it was disclosed that two of the requested tapes were missing—and that one tape had a mysterious 18-minute gap in the middle of a critical conversation.

Battle of the Tapes
—Part II

The House Judiciary Committee on February 6, 1974, received the authority from the full House of Representatives to look into whether there were reasonable grounds to impeach the President, that is, accuse him of wrongdoing in office. This Committee on April 11, 1974, subpoenaed forty-two tapes, searching for evidence of Presidential misconduct.

Then in a surprise move, President Nixon released 1,200 pages of edited transcripts of talks with his aides between September 15, 1972, and April 27, 1973. The President claimed these printed transcripts should once and for all clear him of any connection with the Watergate affair.

Instead of vindicating the President, the tapes made him and his aides sound tough and insensitive. The existence of vulgar language, although deleted, offended millions who read portions of these transcripts published in the country's newspapers. There was incriminating evidence, as well as a portrayal of a President who was indecisive, lacking a concern for the public interest, and apparently ignorant of many simple legal principles.

The House Judiciary Committee rejected the transcripts as insufficient compliance with their subpoena. Its members realized they could not go to court since courts had no jurisdiction in an impeachment proceeding. They decided to go ahead with their investigation without the materials requested. The committee proceeded to conduct a slow but thorough investigation in open sessions on television.

Jaworski
Requests Tapes

In the meantime a grand jury of the United States District Court in Washington, DC, charged seven Watergate defendants with conspiracy to defraud the government and with obstructing justice. The defendants included most of Nixon's top aides and their assistants. Richard Nixon was also named as an unindicted coconspirator. Arrangements were made earlier with John Dean and some others to have them plead guilty to relatively minor charges. This agreement was made in exchange for their future cooperation as government witnesses.

The defendants in the Watergate case were now demanding access to tapes that they claimed would prove their innocence. Special Prosecutor Jaworski was therefore put in a difficult position. If he did not produce the tapes the government could be accused of withholding evidence. Perhaps the case against the Watergate defendants would be dropped. He therefore asked President Nixon for sixty-four more tapes. The President refused to surrender them.

The Special Prosecutor then obtained a subpoena from Federal District Court Judge John Sirica ordering Nixon "to surrender them to the prosecutor." Again the President declined, claiming the Executive Office could not function properly without the ability to conduct affairs of state in private. Giving up the tapes would impair that practice for himself and future occupants of the White House, he claimed.

The District Judge then set 4:00 P.M. Friday, May 24, 1974, as the deadline for the President's lawyer, James St. Clair, to appeal for a ruling by the Court of Appeals of the District of Columbia. Earlier St. Clair had asked Judge Sirica to quash the subpoena, arguing the President was immune from such court orders. Nixon's lawyer argued that this was not a matter for the courts to decide since it was a dispute within the executive branch—between the Special Prosecutor and the President who appointed him. Judge Sirica rejected this and other claims, particularly one of absolute (unlimited) executive privilege. He cited the 1973 Court of Appeals prior ruling concerning the tapes as the reason.

Jaworski, impatient for a decision in the case, did an unusual thing. On May 24 he asked the United States Supreme Court to review the case before it went to the Court of Appeals. "It is of imperative public importance that this case be resolved as quickly as possible to permit the trial in the Watergate cover-up case," stated Jaworski.

The White House opposed Jaworski's request, arguing he should first proceed to the Court of Appeals and that it would be better "that it be decided wisely than that it be decided hurriedly." The Supreme Court agreed to review the case on May 31. Oral arguments were to be heard on June 8.

The Case before
the Supreme Court

The oral arguments before the Supreme Court took almost three hours and were peppered with over 350 questions, mostly directed at James St. Clair, the President's lawyer. At one point in the arguments St. Clair said it was important for the President to get candid communications from anyone, particularly when he was considering Presidential appointments. St. Clair further argued that executive privilege was broad and absolute and would even protect from disclosure Presidential conversations related to criminal conspiracy.

Leon Jaworski argued that the President in refusing to produce the evidence sought by a subpoena in the criminal trial of the seven defendants was interpreting the Constitution as providing the executive branch with special concessions. Jaworski continued, "Now, the President may be right in how he reads the Constitution. But he may also be wrong. And if he is wrong, who is to tell him so? And if there is no one, then the President, of course, is free to pursue his course of erroneous interpretations. What then becomes of our constitutional form of government?. . ." Jaworski was echoing Chief Justice John Marshall's reasoning in the establishment of the power of judicial review.

The Conference

The eight justices of the Supreme Court met the next morning after the oral arguments. One of the justices had disqualified himself earlier. Justice Rehnquist had served under John Mitchell in the Justice Department. Former Attorney General Mitchell was now one of the Watergate defendants.

The justices discussed the case for six hours. But then it took the next two weeks to prepare the opinion. The decision in *United States* versus *Nixon,* as it was officially called, was announced on July 24, 1974.

The Decision

At 11:03 precisely Wednesday morning the cry of the marshall, "Oyez, oyez, oyez," alerted the jammed Supreme Court courtroom that the eight justices were about to appear. Some of the audience of lawyers, Washington notables, and members of the public had waited in line since early the previous afternoon to listen to this ruling on the tapes.

Chief Justice Warren E. Burger, a Nixon appointee, shuffled his papers behind the massive mahogany bench and in a calm, almost icy tone, read the decision. It was a 31-page unanimous 8-0 ruling, which decided that President Nixon must produce for Judge Sirica the tapes of the 64 White House conversations sought by Leon Jaworski. The High Court recognized he needed them in the upcoming obstruction of justice trial of the seven former White House aides.

The Supreme Court rejected the President's argument that the executive branch was entitled under the Constitution to determine the limits of "executive privilege." The Court emphatically reminded everyone that the judicial power to interpret the law "can no more be shared with the Executive branch than the Chief Executive, for example, can share with the Judiciary the veto power, or the Congress share with the judiciary the power to over-ride a presidential veto." The Court quoted directly from the *Marbury* versus *Madison* decision, saying "it is emphatically the province and the duty of the judicial department to say what the law is," particularly in respect to the scope of privilege presented in this case.

Warren Burger, Chief Justice during the
Watergate affair, who read the unanimous
decision setting limits to "executive privilege."
AP/Wide World Photos

The Special Prosecutor, the decision further explained, has the right to subpoena the President even though he is technically an appointee of the President. "The unique facts of this case" do not make this an ordinary intrabranch dispute. The Special Prosecutor was given "unique authority and tenure" to prosecute in the Watergate case. The President also agreed that the Prosecutor would only be removed by consent of Congressional leaders. He therefore has "explicit power to contest the invocation [calling on] of executive privilege in the process of seeking evidence deemed relevant to the performances of these specifically delegated duties."

About one-third of the decision was devoted to the question of executive privilege. President Nixon had based most of his case on this question. The Court agreed that a President is involved in "a vastly wider range of sensitive material than would be true of any ordinary individual [and] it is therefore necessary in the public interest to afford presidential confidentiality the greatest protection consistent with the fair administration of justice." The Supreme Court then elaborated on the necessity for confidentiality but not in an absolute or unlimited way. "A president and those who assist him must be free to explore alternatives in the process of shaping policies and making decisions and to do so in a way many would be unwilling to express except privately. These are the considerations justifying a presumptive privilege for presidential communications. The privilege is fundamental to the operation of government and is inextricably rooted in the separation of powers under the Constitution."

But the Court claimed there are limits to this privilege. The High Court suggested that there are general conditions or circumstances under which the President might claim unlimited executive privilege. Such circumstances might be in order to protect military, diplomatic, or sensitive national security secrets.

The Court quickly explained though that "neither the doctrine of separation of powers, nor the need for confidentiality of high level communications . . . can sustain an absolute, unqualified presidential privilege of immunity from judicial process under all circumstances."

The justices felt the case involving the criminal trial of the Watergate Seven was one of those exceptions. "The allowance of the privilege to withhold evidence that is demonstrably relevant in a criminal trial would cut deeply into the guarantee of due process of law and gravely impair the basic function of the courts." The Court mentioned that "without access to specific facts, a criminal prosecution may be totally frustrated." The justices felt that the Presidential request of unlimited privilege on no more than a generalized claim of public interest in confidentiality of nonmilitary and nondiplomatic discussions, "would upset the constitutional balance of a 'workable government' and greatly impair the role of the courts. . . ."

So in this historic decision the United States Supreme Court was warning future Presidents that even they are not above the law and in a narrow way set forth limits on the power of the Executive Office in areas never before covered. Also in a straightforward way the Supreme Court in this case reaffirmed some basic principles, that it is the sole province of the courts to interpret the Constitution and that defendants have basic rights to a fair trial.

The Resignation
of Richard Nixon

The Court ordered the President to surrender the tapes and materials subpoenaed by Watergate Special Prosecutor Leon Jaworski "forthwith." Nixon's immediate reaction was to refuse to comply with the decision. He had to be convinced that such noncompliance with the High Court's ruling would certainly lead to his impeachment by the House Judiciary Committee. The Committee began four days of public televised debates the very same day the tape decision was announced by the United States Supreme Court. They were about to vote on three articles of impeachment—(1) obstruction of justice, (2) abuse of Presidential authority, and (3) subverting the Constitution by defying eight subpoenas for tapes in order to block impeachment.

St. Clair also threatened that legal ethics would not permit him to stay on as the President's lawyer if he defied the Supreme Court. So only eight hours after the Supreme Court ruling in the *United States* versus *Nixon* case and only one-half hour before the House Judiciary Committee was to meet to debate impeachment charges—St. Clair announced the White House would abide by the Supreme Court ruling.

Judge Sirica, in order to prevent any further stalling by the White House, ordered St. Clair to listen to the tapes personally and comply with a timetable in turning them over to the Special Prosecutor. The President's lawyer was shocked when he listened to the tapes. He immediately realized that the President's fate was now sealed. On June 23, 1972, the President had recorded three conversations with H. R. Haldeman. This was less than a week after the Watergate break-in and only one day after Nixon had assured the nation no one in the White House had been involved in the affair.

The tapes clearly showed that Nixon ordered the C.I.A. to abort the Watergate investigation. This was the clearest piece of evidence demonstrating obstruction of justice by the President of the United States. It was an impeachable offense.

In the meantime the House Judiciary Committee had debated and approved the three articles of impeachment against the President and was prepared to present the case to the entire House of Representatives. If the House voted for impeachment the case would then go to the Senate for trial. In the days immediately following the release of the transcript, Republican leaders met with the President and told him impeachment in the House and conviction by the Senate were now almost certain.

On the evening of August 8, Nixon announced his resignation before a nationwide radio and television audience. The next morning

Secretary of State Henry Kissinger received this note:

Dear Mr. Secretary:
I hereby resign the office of President of the United States.

Sincerely,
(Signed) Richard Nixon

President Gerald Ford, his successor, echoed the emotional relief of the nation when he said: "The long national nightmare is over."

United States versus *Nixon*
Evaluated

The United States Supreme Court in the case *United States* versus *Nixon* concluded that a President in office is not immune from criminal investigation. In making this decision the nation's highest court reaffirmed some of the most basic principles in our American legal system—as well as recognizing a new one. In this decision the Court once again relied on its right to decide according to the Constitution the balance of power in the government.

President Richard Nixon announced his
resignation over nationwide television,
August 8, 1974. AP/Wide World Photos

President Nixon felt very strongly that the branch of government whose constitutional responsibilities are "more gravely affected" should be the ultimate judge of its own actions. Any other way would alter the constitutional balance between the separate and independent legislative, executive, and judicial branches. Warren Burger, quoting John Marshall in his decision, thought otherwise: ". . . it is emphatically the duty of the judicial department to say what the law is." That is why many legal experts in reading this case felt strongly that it was a significant extension of the *Marbury* versus *Madison* decision, which took place one hundred and seventy-one years before. The Court was once again the final arbiter of the meaning of the Constitution.

The case of the *United States* versus *Nixon* also reaffirmed the promise of the Bill of Rights that defendants in criminal trials would get fair trials and that due process would prevail. Special Prosecutor Leon Jaworski needed the Nixon tapes to be used as evidence in the criminal trial of former White House aides. They were charged with attempting to obstruct justice by covering up White House involvement in the Watergate break-in at the Democratic National Headquarters. The lawyers of these defendants felt that the conversations on these tapes might exonerate their clients. The Court ruled that the withholding of such evidence that is demonstrably relevant in a criminal trial would cut deeply into the guarantee of due process of law and gravely impair the basic function of the courts.

A further significance of this case's ruling is that in addition to being a major gain for judicial authority, it in a strange way extended executive power. And it did this by breaking new ground. For the first time in our legal history the justices unanimously recognized a constitutional basis for executive privilege. The Court recognized this right for the office of the Presidency because this office was involved with a "vastly wider range of sensitive material than would be true of any ordinary individual.

"A President has a definite right to keep his conversations and correspondence confidential just as all citizens have a right to privacy. This privilege is fundamental to the operation of government and is inextricably rooted in the separation of powers under the Constitution." The Court also declared that in many areas, for example, "military, diplomatic or sensitive national security secrets," the President has constitutional support for confidentiality. He may even go to court to defend this right. But none of these rights is absolute; the courts in the future may put restrictions on this

119

privilege. This is what the Court did in this case in the area involving criminal procedures.

Nixon in the text of his speech accepting the tapes decision recognized the new principle when he stated: "For the future, it will be essential that the special circumstances of this case not be permitted to cloud the rights of Presidents to maintain the basic confidentiality without which this office cannot function. I was gratified, therefore, to note that the Court reaffirmed both the validity and the importance of the principle of executive privilege."

The Burger Court was wise enough to check this President but not tie the hands of future Chief Executives. Perhaps the greatest significance of this decision is that the two-hundred-year-old document—the Constitution—had worked. It had provided the legal and peaceful way to stop the encroachment of power by a twentieth-century head of government.

The Living Constitution

John Marshall's prophecy that the Constitution was "intended to endure for the ages . . . and consequently to be adapted to the various crises in human affairs," has so far been true. It is now the world's oldest written constitution and is entering its third century of service to our country. We have in this book spanned the last two hundred years of America's history and have seen the Constitution called upon in three periods of crisis.

But the Constitution, as Justice Potter Stewart stated, is not "a self-executing document." What brought the Constitution to life and made it a human document was the fulfillment of the role sketched out in it for the judiciary branch. The United States Supreme Court in particular played a major role in bringing the meaning of the Constitution to life. One hundred and four justices, from John Jay to the nine justices on the Court today, have had the right to say what the Constitution means.

In 1803 in the case of *Marbury* versus *Madison* the Court took on this role as the "final arbiter of the meaning of the Constitution." John Marshall stated in this landmark decision that "it is emphatically the province and duty of the judicial department to say what the law is." This was the first time in our country's history that this constitutional principle was so forcefully stated. Without this pronouncement the survival of the Constitution might have been questionable. If it had been left to each branch of government to decide whether it was following the mandates of the Constitution, the document might have been torn to shreds. The interpretation of the Constitution was not meant to be left to political bargaining. *Marbury* versus *Madison* established the right of an independent judiciary to evaluate the acts of the other two branches of government. As we have seen, the authors of the Constitution intended the life terms of the justices to give them independence from political influences.

In 1857 the United States Supreme Court for the second time declared a law of Congress unconstitutional. It claimed that this branch of the federal government through the passage of the Missouri Compromise in 1820 had overstepped its constitutional bounds. Unfortunately the Court was itself caught up in partisanship over the question of slavery. It reached its decision in response to political pressures and dealt itself a "self-inflicted wound" from which it took decades to recover. The decision was received with outrage by the antislavery forces and contributed to the growing division between North and South. Although the Court may have thought it could prevent further division in the country, in only four years war broke out.

In 1974 the country was faced with the executive branch of government misusing power and ignoring some of our most fundamental principles of law. In the case of *United States* versus *Nixon* the Court ruled that even Presidents are not above the law and their powers are not absolute. Again the Supreme Court drew from the wellspring of the Constitution.

President Nixon resigned from his high office on August 9, 1974. The vice president, Gerald Ford, was sworn into the office of President, and the government survived the crisis. The two-hundred-year-old Constitution had again buoyed up the country.

For Further Reading

Marbury versus *Madison*

Beveridge, Albert J. *The Life of John Marshall.* Boston: Berg, 1916.

Fribourg, Marjorie. *The Supreme Court In American History.* New York: Avon Books, 1965.

Smith, Margaret B. *The First Forty Years of Washington Society.* New York: Scribner and Sons, 1906.

Warren, Charles. *The Supreme Court in United States History.* Boston: Little Brown, 1935.

Dred Scott Decision

Fehrenbacher, Don. *Slavery, Law and Politics, The Dred Scott Case in Historical Perspective.* New York: Oxford University Press, 1978.

Filler, Louis. *The Crusade Against Slavery, 1830-1860.* New York: Harper and Row, 1960.

Franklin, John Hope. *From Slavery to Freedom, A History of Negro Americans.* 3rd ed. New York: Alfred A. Knopf, 1967.

Kutler, Stanley. *The Dred Scott Decision, Law or Politics.* Boston: Houghton Mifflin, 1967.

Latham, Frank B. *The Dred Scott Decision.* New York: Franklin Watts, 1968.

Pfeffer, Leo. *This Honorable Court*. Boston: Beacon Press, 1965.

Swisher, Carl B. *Roger B. Taney*. New York: Macmillan, 1936.

United States versus Nixon

Costello, William. *The Facts About Nixon*. New York: Viking Press, 1960.

Magruder, Jeb Stuart. *An American Life: One Man's Road to Watergate*. New York: Atheneum, 1974.

McKown, Robin. *The Resignation of Nixon, A Dedicated President Gives Up the Nation's Highest Office*. New York: Franklin Watts, 1975.

The New York Times. *The End of a Presidency*. New York: Bantam Books, 1974.

Osbourne, John. *The Nixon Watch*. New York: Liveright, 1970.

Sussman, Barry. *The Great Coverup: Nixon and the Scandal of Watergate*. New York: New American Library, 1974.

Index

INDEX

About the Author

Peter Sgroi is a free-lance writer and resides in West Nyack, New York, with his wife, Mary Anne, and their teenage son and daughter, Peter and M.J. In addition to his law and historical book contributions to juvenile literature, he has written articles for national magazines. Presently he is teaching Advanced Placement American History and Constitutional Law in one of the Westchester County, New York, schools.